# Bi-Cultural

Living and Leaving the World of Illusion

by

Mus Zoser Ankh Hat

OVOLR! / DEBACKLE
RICHMOND, VIRGINIA
USA

ISBN: 978-0-9986977-8-9

Library of Congress Control Number: 2020932190

Copyright 2020

Mus Zoser Ankh Hat
Atlanta, Georgia

"Babylon system is the vampire,
Suckin' the children day by day,
Me say: de Babylon system is the vampire,
falling empire,
Suckin' the blood of the sufferers
Building church and university,
Deceiving the people continually,
Me say them graduatin' thieves and murderers"

Babylon System~
The Honorable Robert Nesta Marley

# Acknowledgments

I would first like to give honor and reverence to The All because without you nothing would exist. I would also like to show my love and respect to the Great Mother. Like I said many times, I handed in my "patriarchal card" a long time ago. I overstand and acknowledge that you are the Great Mother of creation and on this physical plane you are our provider, nurturer, protector, teacher and friend. I would like to give thanks to Paa Nabab Yaanuwn for his sacrifice and for giving us an example of what we need to be as individuals and as a collective. I would also like to thank Etwal Bwiye Bon Mambo for linking me to the spirits that guide and protect me. I want to give thanks to Priestess Auset Ra Amen for her guidance and to my ancestors known and unknown for guiding and protecting me on this life cycle. Lastly, I thank Joyce, my friends, and family for putting up with me on my journey. Without you all, I would not be the person I am.

# Foreword

The people of America, within their various demographics, have the social and constitutional ability to constantly change and welcome different cultures and perspectives across regions in the nation. An important aspect of this cultural acceptance is acknowledging the differing experiences we had growing up in separate areas of this large country. As such, I wrote this book for the people that have not only experienced growing up in the Caucasian American suburbia but also for the people that never had the experience—The people of color that never stepped foot out the hood and never had to deal with being submerged into Caucasian American culture. This book is also for Caucasians that are curious about the lives of those few minorities they spent time with during school, work, or even within their neighborhoods. While I want this work to challenge the reader to understand how this blend of cultures can affect the psyche of individuals, the reader should also understand that this is not an Anti-American book. I was born in this country and, as of now, it's the only country I know. I've seen the good, the bad, and the ugly here and appreciate all the experiences that this country has given me. Instead, this book refers to being a black American man and living in a system that has been made for you to ultimately be a negro or a nigger. You're either going to jail or you're a paid "slave" helping to put building blocks onto the American dream I recognize as an illusion. The system teaches Black American citizens to love Jesus, go to school, get a job, get married, have kids and eventually own a house with a white picket fence. What happens when this American Dream is challenged? When the foreign religion and history we were raised on is questioned, and we learn to use our God given talents to benefit ourselves? Doubting the American dream can erect memories of traditions that have been long forgotten and erase the illusion we've been conditioned to accept. This is the story of how I overcame the illusion—how a young man battled the trials and tribulations of Caucasion suburban America to gain the true title of being an African-minded individual living in America. I am Bi-cultural.

# Introduction

Cycles are never ending. Inside these cycles of time comes evolution, reconstruction, destruction and a midst of other natural occurrences. As a part of these processes, hybrids, deformities, and a host of other specimens are cultivated within these conditions. The Black American is a byproduct of these cycles as well. The modern day Black American is a result of these cycles being temporarily interrupted, causing regression to a point in which they have lost total recollection of their culture, spiritual systems, language, and ancient esoteric disciplines. These cycles have put the Black American at the lower evolutionary scale of this modern day society. This book talks about a personal journey of an individual that has been able to live a two-part life. He was groomed and molded by a system that is not made for him or his own people; a system designed to wash clean his true world history and self identity. American societies have created a nation in which living free is not as truthful as it sounds. A nation devoid of individuality that trains us to be worker bees charged with finding a good job, staying out of debt, and dying with enough material possessions to leave something for their families before moving on. This is not what life is about. Tough times and wonderful experiences came with the path I travelled to become the man I am today. And on that path, I discovered life is about being Bi-cultural: living two separate cultures within one reality.

# I

# The Rebirth of Zo

During a cold winter day on December 16, in the small town of Cheverly Maryland, I came into this world. I was received by two hard working and loving parents. A mother working as an x-ray file room manager and a father that owned his own carpentry business. During that time, we were considered mid-to-upper class. I lived in a Cape Cod style house, went to catholic school, had a role as an altar boy, was a boy scout, and played sports. It should be noted that despite my role as an altar boy, I was never felt up by a priest, or had any other heinous acts committed against me by church actors. On the contrary, life was good. It was the 80's and my world revolved around going to school, being an altar boy, playing with my diverse group of friends, and watching MTV. Little did I know, MTV would become the foundation of me eventually becoming a "Black Rocker", but as a child it only served as entertainment. In school, I remember wearing the plaid uniform and my teachers and principal being nuns. As an altar boy, I remember looking at the religious statues and paintings, and the voice inside my head telling me that something wasn't right. Regardless of these feelings, this was the life my parents wanted me to lead, and I respected their decision.

Aside from religion, sports was also a key aspect of my life. Sports taught me to be competitive, but also made me realize I did not like to lose. I dabbled in soccer, but my main focus was baseball. Mainly, because my dad took us to many Orioles and Colts games. When I was eight years old, I remember seeing 'Ole Sweetness', Walter Payton play on a snowy afternoon. The Colts were terrible, and the fans were throwing snowballs at them. In the pregame, I remember looking everywhere for Mr. Payton, then watching in awe as he came out in a cut-off t-shirt despite the below-freezing weather. To this day, I swear he was either a God or superman: I couldn't believe what I was looking at. Once the game started, he ran for one-hundred and thirty-four yards, scoring a few touchdowns. It was a big sports moment for me. The other moment that stands out from that time was watching the 1983 World Series from my grandmother's house, and seeing Cal Ripken Jr catch that line drive, earning the championship title for Baltimore.

I mentioned previously the impacts MTV had on my musical tastes. I was first introduced to the channel when various circumstances made it so I wasn't allowed to go outside, either due to punishment, or bad weather. It was amazing to see all the different styles of music and all the imagery that came along with those videos. I loved my MTV, from Prince and Michael Jackson to Duran Duran—it influenced me in so many ways. This was a time when unfortunately, the programming along with other TV shows, never really portrayed black people in an uplifting light. My main heroes of color were either musicians or sports heroes. We didn't have any Black Panther movies then, so I cheered on characters like Superman and Rocky who didn't resemble me at all. I knew I was black, but I was mainly exposed to the Caucasian imagery of what a 'hero' is. I was just like that ad with the little black boy, looking in the mirror and seeing a white superman figure. Regardless, I'll say this: I absolutely loved everything about the 80's. Especially because I didn't have to get a job and I was able to live my life free as a child that didn't have a care in the world. Racism, as an everyday occurrence, hadn't been introduced to me yet. I just remember a few blatant episodes: My brother and I were in line getting popcorn at JCPenney's, and after we bought it, this old white man reached in the popcorn and started eating it. Another incident was at the community center; they were handing out refreshments and this old Italian woman tried to refuse us drinks. Granted, she looked like some of those beat up old battle axes off the godfather. Like I said, my friends were of all colors, so I saw no colors at all. My life just really consisted of 3 major things: Priests, sports and MTV. This is what molded me and prepared me for the next phase of life.

# 2

# Da Wonder Years

When I was around 9 years old, we moved briefly to Texas, but ended up in Virginia. The story on that is simple: My dad worked outside and saw a man fall off the roof and die, to which he responded "hell naw" to that Texas heat. We moved to a lower middle-class section right outside of Richmond, Virginia. Yes indeed, good ole Richmond Virginia, the capital of the confederacy. Of course, at the time, none of that mattered. I just remember being able to play football for the first time, and baseball got more competitive. I was the new boy at Henning elementary, and within the first week, I got into a fight with a guy. I found out afterwards that he was actually the 'school bully', when, following the fight, a whole slew of people whispered in my ear, "He deserved that," and, "Way to go." This new school is where things started to take a slight turn to my introduction to race. My teacher, Mr. Sword, started teaching about slavery. I remember everyone looking at the black people in class and feeling terrible. I raised my hand and said, "Were their white slaves too?" Mr. Sword said yes, and went on to talk about indentured servants.

There was a guy in my class named Danny that always seemed to get attention from the girls. One day I approached him and said, "Man! How do you do it!?" He was white, of course, and considering I was colorblind I didn't have a clue to how all of this worked. He told me to watch him and he somehow managed to get close to all the girls while they were sitting down. I thought he was the coolest guy ever. There was this Aryan queen I liked, named Michelle. Since they were friends, Danny decided to help me out. We rode our bikes to her house and knocked on the door, only to be greeted by the Aryan queen herself. "Here he is!" Danny presented me happily, but she wasn't very receptive. "WHAT?! SO?! I'm eating dinner so I have to go!" She said, before slamming the door in our faces. Obviously, the Aryan queen did not want anything to do with jungle fever. This kind of situation happened to me again and again, in many different ways, until around the time I left Richmond as a young adult. I liked women but the choices of Nubian goddesses were very low. Regardless of that, life was just swell.

My parents decided to have us spend our summers in Maryland, and would drop us off in Baltimore, in Edmondson village. Being West Baltimore, it wasn't the roughest, but it was a far cry from Cheverly and Richmond. I thought I was a little tough from fighting all the time in Richmond, but I got mopped up good in Baltimore a few times. One evening, me and my cousins were walking down the street, right near the alleys, when these boys suddenly came out. They knew my cousins, but we were new so they started mouthing off. My older cousin de-escalated the situation, but one boy said to my cousin, "I'm not going to fight you…" then looked at me and said, "…But Him!!!" Needless to say, I got my first good ass whooping that day. I quickly adapted to life in 'B-more', as we called it, and I saw some new things. I started to notice, and have fonder liking for females because they were all over the place. I also was exposed to some homosexuality that I didn't really understand until I got older. Again, I didn't get boofed, but I saw some things described as 'Boys being Boys'. I was exposed to welfare, and to people that didn't live like we lived back home. This was an eye opener but as a kid there's a tendency to just go with the flow. Still there was nothing too bad. I was disappointed a few times, but nothing earth shattering. I do remember getting a spanking when I was in JCPenney because I wanted a Michael Jackson fake "diamond studded" glove, and decided to stage a protest at the register. I promptly got mopped up, leaving me with my Mickey Mouse watch broken, and no Mj glove.

After a while of living outside Richmond, My family moved to Midlothian, Virginia; a suburb to the south of the city. My neighborhood had a few other black families, so it didn't seem so different from Maryland but, relatively speaking, it was almost night and day. This didn't become so apparent to me until a bit later, probably because I was good at sports, so I was always treated a little different to a certain degree. I still loved baseball, and my friend Antwone and I were the biggest baseball geeks in the world. My life at that time was baseball and collecting baseball cards with friends, football, and playing Nintendo. Again, a good life. It was pretty much smooth sailing until high school came. Now, my friends, this is when it gets interesting.

# 3

# "JUST SHUT UP YOU BLACK NIGGER!!!"

During my freshman year in high school, I was one of the youngest kids in the class. I was still playing little league football as a freshman while most of my friends were on the junior varsity team. In this new high school, Midlothian, they combined the districts so that the rich people, who lived on one side of the tracks, and everyone else, went to the same school. Across the tracks was an affluent neighborhood, called Salisbury. The houses the white boys and girls lived in looked like mansions to me. We, however, lived in a modest ranch home, on the other side of the tracks.

In high school, I started noticing something odd with my youth teammates: They tended to distance themselves from me. While this was confusing to me at first, I didn't think much of it. Unfortunately, due to my grades, I couldn't play baseball in my freshman year, which was heartbreaking. But I made the team the following year as the result of a lot of hard work. I was ecstatic. However, there was a setback: My best friend, Antwone, quit playing baseball due to an incident with his teammates. At an end of season practice, one of the white boys used the eye black, (a grease applied under the eyes to prevent glare from the sun) to make himself into black face, and proceeded to make an onslaught of racist jokes. I didn't take it seriously, but Antwone never played again after that. This meant I was alone. Soon after, Antwone moved across town. I found a few new friends who were mainly white. Despite the move, Antwone and I still hung out. Antwone now lived in one of the nice houses. So we formed a little crew with the neighborhood boys in his area. I'd ride my bike to his house, and we'd play Sega Genesis, Madden, listen to music, watch movies, and just have a good time. I was still naive to what the world was presenting to me, but I was about to get a wakeup call.

It happened when my friends and I were playing around at the local fitness gym called Briarwood. I remember roasting my boy Scott really harshly, to the point where he almost started crying. His response however, instead of roasting me back, was to shout, "JUST SHUT UP YOU BLACK NIGGER!" I looked at him with a mix of confusion and hurt while all of the other guys went quiet and just looked at me. That was the day that I realized I was different from everyone else. Unfortunately, I had to get used to being called names like: Black Nigger, Porch Monkey, Joe Coon, Cotton picker, Black bastard, Nigger, and pretty much every other racist name imaginable. Imagine dealing with this treatment on an almost daily basis. Going into parties, and drunk white boys saying, "Who invited this NIGGER? We don't want you here! Get the fuck out of here you fucking NIGGER!!!" I remember walking into a party and from a group of white boys playing cards, one said, "Good! There is my LUCKY NIGGER." Instead of defending me, most of the people there just laughed. I didn't understand what I did wrong, or why I was being treated that way.

Incidents like this became more frequent the more I became aware of them. I remember nooses being left on my football locker, and racist people yelling 'nigger' when I rode my bike down the street. One of the harshest wake up calls to me occured when I was at my job, at Chick-Fil-A: An older, white male co-worker said, "You see this white cutting board? This is the closest you'll ever be to being white!" My new reality was about being a black boy surrounded by racist, and ignorant, teens, adults, teachers, and police.

Thinking back, sometimes it's hard to believe the shit I went through. My lovelife was non-existent. I only got the scraps of the below-average looking white girls that were curious about me. I had a crush on an Irish girl, but her parents were both racist. In the end, I went to prom alone. At multiple points, I recall looking in the mirror and saying to myself, "Damn I wish I was white! Things would be so much easier." I had completely assimilated to the suburban white culture and mindset that surrounded me. This assimilation led to me being called 'Oreo' by the few black students who were Afro Centric, and were embracing the message spread throughout the nineties about black consciousness. I couldn't relate at the time.

My love of sports encouraged me to endure the teasing and torment, and I made it out of high school partially intact. A part of me had given in to the pressures of living in that reality. There were so many stories I made up just to make my parents seem richer. Once I lied about where I lived by having a teammate's mother drop me off at a nicer looking house. The illusion had become a reality to me, and I wanted nothing more than to be a part of the white, American dream. Eventually people caught on to the lies and, needless to say, it wasn't a good look. All of this, just to be accepted by people that hated me because of the color of my skin.

# 4

# The Awakening

After I made it out of high school my whole life changed. I was exposed to an array of new things. First, I went to work at a local sandwich shop with some of the illest cats in that area. It was here that I learned how to sell and smoke weed. I was also introduced to punk rock music, after my high school graduation, at an annual event known as 'Beach Week'. On the beach, we were listening to the radio and someone put in a greatest hits album by The Ramones. It had all of their classics like, 'Sheena was a Punk Rocker', 'Beat on the Brat', and many others I would come to learn. The music really spoke to me. It was fast, loud, and angry, just like I was at that point in my life. My treatment in high school had left me pissed off, with no reasonable outlet to express myself, so this music provided the relief I needed. This attachment to punk rock was only increased after I visited a local band with my childhood friend, Lawrence. He was a white boy that had recently moved back to Richmond from Atlanta, and, despite our racial difference, we related to each other very well. We fell back in together tight. During a local Battle of the Bands show, we saw a band play called Broken Chains of Segregation. To me, it sounded like a hardcore version of Rage Against the Machine. I remember watching them play and immediately thinking, "I want to do that," so I went to the local record shop, and put up a flyer to find other musicians. With this act, I came to know four of the coolest white dudes I've ever met. We started rehearsing constantly until we got good, and began playing shows enough to the point where we began to get known locally. This, inadvertently, changed my status with the women I would meet, and I went from being seen as an ugly black boy to being somewhat desirable. I finally was able to link up with good-looking women, and felt like I was no longer the creature from the black lagoon. Despite my upgraded romantic situations, I was still angry with the world around me. But I was able to release it all, through my music, by screaming, yelling, cursing, and speaking my own version of the truth. We called the band Indypendant. We came together as friends, and became a family that had each other's backs. Race was never an issue with us; we were humans that cared for each other. To this day, I still speak to them all. The Richmond, Virginia hardcore scene became a sanctuary for me. I met liked-minded individuals and, with the exception of a few racist encounters, we all got along.

It was a common occurrence for all the same kids to go to the record store and get a hardcore punk album and a Wutang clan album the same day. I learned there, that the Richmond hardcore scene is amazing, and I was introduced to my fellow "black rockers." These guys were all older than me, and schooled me on bands like Bad Brains, 24-7 spyz, Fishbone, Steel Pulse and all the other relevant Black Rock and Reggae bands. They also taught me valuable lessons about women, politics, racism and life. They were aware of their blackness and were very deep in their 'black conscious' studies. These brothers took me in and groomed me to be the black rocker I would eventually evolve into.

The next sequence of events in my life play an extremely beneficial role in the evolution of my story, and explain how being exposed to the world can broaden one's perspective. It may sound like a pity party at first, but that couldn't be further from the truth.

When I graduated high school, I went to a community college in the city. Being away from the normal people I went to high school with, it was a somewhat new experience. I remember taking an African American studies class, which was a considerably new concept to me. In this class, I had a professor who was esteemed in her field, and well-liked by both her students and staff. She was the typical accomplished Black American. She and her husband went to the best schools, lived in the suburbs, and went to an all-white church. At the time it was kind of confusing; she wasn't like Angela Davis or anyone like that, but she was a good Black American teacher and person. I had an all black class in which we usually held discussions, and read all the classic African American books. Reading these books started to change my mind about how I viewed myself as Black American. One incident made me realize how badly I was brainwashed and how much self-hatred I had towards myself and my people. In one of our discussions, the teacher mentioned how black women were portrayed, expressing "You know how they see us black women." I went on to comment, "Dirty, ugly, smelly and stupid!" And a host of other self-hating comments. I'm certain it went beyond the self-hate, and a real hate of black women spouted out of me like it was coming out of a neo-nazi or klan member. Thankfully a few of my classmates laughed, because they didn't believe I was being serious. Unfortunately, I was. When I finished speaking, I realized how bad my brainwashing had become but I didn't know what to do about it.

I landed my first official job at the First North American National Bank as a credit card bill collector. A few of my friends had landed a gig there and put me on. I had a lesbian manager that was cool, and I incidentally made her favorites list when I made the team sign a rainbow (I had no actual knowledge of the Pride flag, so this was purely coincidence). As always, there were not many Blacks servicing the bank.

At work, I sat across from a brother named Taqi, and a sister named Kenya who was pregnant at the time. I used my knowledge from my African American studies class to engage them in conversations and debates, which usually led to me asking a lot of questions and getting roasted a lot by Kenya. She was a proud Nubian conscious sister who wore head wraps and had a good energy overall. We discussed Jews one time and my naive and ignorant ass was like, "Jews are the most persecuted people!" Kenya looked at me and said, "Negro please," then proceeded to go on a 5 minute educational display of knowledge that I can't say I've ever seen before from a black person, and definitely not a woman. She schooled my ass and I came away feeling like the biggest lowlife on the planet. Her lesson came at the right time though. I had recently left the catholic church, determined to be a Rastafarian and search for the truth. I would always ask questions to Taqi and Kenya, and Taqi always had an answer that made sense. Taqi gave me a scroll (little book) called Our Bondage. It had pictures of biblical people that were black, and bible verses written and translated from the original text: It was amazing! This scroll introduced me to a variety of others that I would read in the following years: works written by Dr. Malachi Z York. I had previously read books by many other great authors like Zechariah Sitchen, Dr Ivan van Sertima, The honorable Elijah Muhammad and Chek Anti Diop. Their ancient knowledge, science, and self-help information were everything to me at this point. The name Mus Zoser Ankh Hat was given to me by Dr. York because he taught me the importance of a meaningful name. The meaning of the name fit me perfectly. I was now a black rocker who liked white women, that was slowly being introduced to Black African culture. A semi-conscious hybrid among a small percentage of people in America. The next move was to get more experience, so I took a semester off and went to London, England.

# 5

# London's Calling

I earned money for my trip to London by cutting grass and delivering pizzas. My friend, Cheeze, was able to connect me with his guy Mark that lived in London, who offered to show me around. As soon as I got off the plane, I was treated to a new world of excitement. While going through Customs, the agent began to ask questions, so many, in fact, I was the only person left from the flight being interrogated. Later on, while watching an airport reality show, I saw the same customs agent kick an Australian back home for having a one-way ticket. Speaking of TV shows, while in London, I was also surprised to see a woman from a show on the Discovery Channel called The Steps to Pregnancy. I greeted her by shouting, "You're the woman from that show!" She responded with a smile and affirmation, but her husband wasn't too thrilled about the interruption.

I got settled in London right away, and experienced jet lag for the first time in my life; It took around a day to overcome. Later, I met up with Mark who introduced me to his wife, roommates, and showed me around the town. Eventually he handed me off to these two brothers named Freddie and Lajoie: French musicians, who lived in a one-bedroom flat in an expensive part of London. One had the bedroom, and the other was sleeping on the couch. We spent our days talking about music, race, and listening to Bob Marley. Yet, despite our conversations, we held no ill-thoughts towards the white people that mistreated us. We had different ways of dealing with racism.

Eventually I had to move to a hostel in Stockwell, which was one train stop from Brixton. It was funny because in order to get to the hostel, I had to walk through the government projects. But considering most people don't have guns in London, I was never afraid of anything happening. They weren't like the projects in America.

At the hostel I got my room and my first roommate was a guy from Poland. Every night, I came home and we would talk to each other until one of us fell asleep. We talked about everything: He told me the first time he saw a black person, and how he thought that if he touched them the color would come off, or that if they jumped in a pool the color would wash away. He wasn't trying to be racist or insult anyone, but he had never experienced it before. He also told me how they loved and worshipped the black Madonna, and it opened my eyes to a new point of view on both people and life. The hostel we were staying at had an open mic night, so I went down one evening and gave it a shot. Partly because I realized that anything a Black American did there, would be amplified to another level. I had no clue that black Americans were looked with something of valued position in Europe. I had gone from the "creature of the black lagoon," to Denzel Washington. My long locks and looks also added onto my value with the ladies. I met a French girl who was curious about me, and this led to a lot of questions before we eventually hooked up. She told me her dad would prefer her to be with a black man, and that her dad was a doctor. This brief encounter helped me overstand how different things were for people of color overseas, versus in America. Another encounter was with a brother that became my second roommate, a refugee from Africa, who finished his schooling in London after he claimed asylum. When he got aid from the government, we would watch movies, eat food, and drink beer.

I eventually moved to Earls Court, which was a few stops down from Wimbledon. In this Hostel, I had a total of five roommates: Two girls from Sweden, a guy from New Zealand, a guy from Australia, and a girl from France. Every night after work, we would all sit around and talk. On one occasion, I remember us talking about race, and I told them about the racism I dealt with growing up in the U.S. Some of the girls became visibly upset, they were confused about the treatment I had received in the States, and they couldn't understand the reasoning behind it. I had originally thought all white people were racist, like the numerous American whites I had encountered, but I learned that this could not have been further from the truth. It took me a while to overstand that all white people aren't racist rednecks from the country. I also encountered people from Germany that weren't racist, but were simultaneously very proud of their heritage. This German guy, who lived in the hostel, was always working on his laptop. One day I saw him at a bar, and started joking with him about being a nazi. He expressed to me, "What Hitler brought to the German people was efficiency!" He then pointed to a bar where there were three bartenders working and asked, "You see that bar right there? They have three bartenders right?" I confirmed and he continued, "What Hitler would have done is had one bartender doing the same job all by himself!!! Hitler was about efficiency!" I was too drunk at the time to debate him, but I could understand his point of view. He was clearly proud of his nation in some regard, but his opinions never came across as anti-semitic or racist. It was just an example of the many different types of people I was exposed to in London, and how they gave me a new perspective on the world.

Low funds persuaded me to look for a gig, and in a week's time I was lucky enough to find one. A French-Canadian man that did the hostel's laundry, said he was leaving, and wanted to know If I needed a job. I gladly took the job, as well as all the benefits that came along with it; which included staying in the hostel for free. I was living the black American celebrity life, and all the people seemed to like me. Among the lot were Australians, South Africans, New Zealanders, and many other nationalities.

One day after work, my co-workers and I decided we should go get drinks. The place was called The Richmond (A funny coincidence). A short while after we entered the bar, I realized that not only was I the only man at the table, but all of the women were looking at me like I was a pork chop on those old cartoons while stranded on a deserted island. An Italian woman kept calling me beautiful at the bar and I noticed all the other women had similar sentiments. I must admit, this fueled my ego quite a bite; in fact, my confidence skyrocketed. This treatment was vastly different than how the white women at home treated me, and I enjoyed every moment of it.

I eventually met a girl from Australia named Stacey. She was traveling with a friend, our paths crossed, and we hooked up then decided to hang out for a while. She told me she was a tennis player and cheerleader back home - everything I desired in high school. And she actually wanted to be with me. She decided to stay in London and got a job, so I crashed at her place frequently instead of living at the hostel. Staying with her was much better than sleeping in the bunk bed with all the other hostel workers. Throughout Stacy and I's interactions, I learned the complications of being Bi-Cultural. While I wasn't interested in seriously dating or marrying a Caucasian woman, my previous conditioning still made them attractive to me. Realistically, I always pictured myself bringing home a Black woman, or at least someone of color, to introduce to my parents. Granted, they wouldn't mind if she were white, since I have four bi-racial nieces and nephews: Racial integration in our family is not an issue. My personal opinion is that, whoever makes you happy, be with them! Same sex, different races, how does your orientation or preferences impact me at all? It doesn't - so if you like it, I love it! Stacey was amazing, but a few incidents with her affirmed my desire of wanting a Black queen. I remember walking through the London zoo with Stacey one day, and when we went by the gorilla section, she teased, "Hey, he looks like you!" I looked at her like she was crazy, and I said something banterful back. That was the end of the conversation. In another situation, she started bashing aborigines in a racist manner. I knew then that Stacey, like other white women, would never truly be able to relate to me.

I became more self-aware though. At the British museum, I was fascinated after seeing all the artifacts I learned about in my studies. African, Summerian, Egyptian, and many more relics of ancient civilizations were all present. This was amazing and instilled in me more confidence in, and conformation of the information I was reading. Soon, my time in London came to an end, but all of the experiences I had there in that brief period of time elevated me to a new personal level. I came back home a different person. I was really starting to get to 'know thyself', and I was ready for the next chapter in life.

# 6

# Back in Black

Things were becoming very confusing at this point in my life, to say the least: I went from not seeing race as an issue, to then having everything flipped over. The uncertainty was immeasurable. I wanted to be a part of a culture that wanted nothing to do with me, and I wanted so desperately to just fit in. Yet, only to be rejected in the worst possible ways. Then, out of nowhere, I learned the true history of my race and how it differed from the lies spread by American schools. But old habits are hard to break. My most recent experiences at the time had launched me into a transitional phase, on a path to become what I truly believed, was "Black." Unfortunately, there's not a black consciousness switch I could flip that would reverse the years of training I had received growing up. I still spoke like the white people I was raised around, still listened to the same music, and still desired white women, though now to a lesser degree. My newfound consciousness filtered all my thoughts and impulses before they were approved. For example, whenever I had the urge to connect with a white woman, I remembered my desire for my future children to have full, wooly hair and deep melanin.

This is the type of mindset I adapted as I returned from London. However, I noticed how drastically things had changed during the 2000s in America. Interracial dating was no longer as taboo as it was while I was in school. This, accompanied with my boosted ego from the trip, was a dangerous combination. I remember visiting my friend Josef at his bar in Richmond, and being approached by these two girls. One was white and the other was Eurasian, but they had both gone to Virginia Tech. I noticed quickly after we started talking that one girl was an Aryan queen. She began complimenting me on aspects of my looks I'd normally be ridiculed for in the states, and she eventually invited me to a party they were both going to. The party was nice, and I saw many of my old classmates. Afterwards, one of the girls invited me back to her place, so I wouldn't have to drive home in my mildly-intoxicated state. As soon as we were settled, I said to the group, "We're all adults here, right?" They agreed. "Okay, I'm sleeping with her," I announced while pointing to the Aryan queen. This elicited a laugh out of everyone but, nonetheless, the Aryan queen left to her bedroom. Tired as I was, I was also interested in seeing where this would go, so I followed her into the bedroom only for her to exit the bathroom wearing nothing but a long sleeve Virginia Tech 'Hokie' shirt, and underwear. I was ready! ... Then the black consciousness filter kicked in and I calmed down my impulses. I ended up not doing anything with her - it was the first time I had resisted being a slave to my past.

While I'd be lying if I said that I didn't hook up with any white women after that, there have been numerous times where I allowed my new filter to guide my decisions rather than my older mindset. This attraction to women outside of my own race didn't really leave me until late adulthood. Now, I'm only attracted to women that can relate to me and most white women don't want to speak about subjects that impact my people and my environment, so it's an easy choice.

Regardless, till this day, I still have friends I talk to back home. I met some good white people while growing up but, in all reality, the ratio of good to bad white people has been lopsided from my experience. However, it's much easier to live without concern of those lopsided odds unless it's necessary.

I usually wait until I've had time to feel a person out before I become comfortable enough to open up to them. I extend this same caution to everyone, but personal experience has taught me to be extra cautious of white people that I don't know. Luckily, I'm good at figuring out people now, and have developed quite a proficient radar.

# 7

# The Black Mecca

There were three major reasons for why I wanted to move to Atlanta: One, I was sick of Richmond; Two, I wanted to get close to the Holy Tabernacle Ministries that owned land in Eatonton, Georgia; Three, my brother was working for Georgia Tech, and I could live with him. After the move, I didn't do much besides study, and get well acquainted with the brothers and sisters of the organization. I did learn about the key differences between Atlanta and Richmond though. On one of my first jobs, I was interviewed by a white guy who was a night-time rocker with a band of his own. He hired me, and I remember immediately seeing a sea of chocolate as soon as I walked out onto the main floor. I realized how beautiful the Nubian goddesses were, and valued the laid back attitude of all the brothers.

I went from a mostly-all-white Virginia, to a multicultural London, and ended up in a very-black Atlanta. Because of this change, I ended up with my first black girlfriend. She was a Black American Nigerian with a child from a previous relationship. We got along well, and the fact she had a child was never an issue. We also worked at the same magazine company, which was a plus. Unfortunately, my inexperience in bed caused rifts in our relationship: while I thought I was making home runs, I was actually striking out. This would have been a problem we could have worked through, however, she tended to gossip about our encounters to our coworkers. Around the same time, I also learned that she was cheating on me with her ex-boyfriend. As karma would have it, I was friends with the manager and she was fired for her behavior. To add insult to injury, her ex-boyfriend also cheated on her once they were back together. In the end, it was an odd relationship that taught me quite a few things and made me into less of an oblivious person. The whole "Nice guys end up last" became a certain reality to me.

Things may not have been going great relationship-wise, but I still had baseball to look forward to. In a city surrounded by my own race, the only contact I had with the white world was through my diverse baseball team. I played in an eighteen-and-up, Men's adult league, but we were all the same age, so most of us connected with each other. One of my most memorable teammates was a guy named Josh that we called, 'Super white boy', due to how fast and abnormally athletic he was. The team was like another mini-family; We would often go out on Sunday nights and get into trouble in Atlanta.

Those nights out were beloved by another unforgettable teammate we called, 'Wretched Rob.' He was a Colombian, who loved to go to strip clubs and had a fetish for dating strippers. For some reason, he always called me up to accompany him to strip clubs, only to hand me money for drinks and disappear into the VIP room. At the time, I didn't really understand the strip club scene and usually spent my time just talking to bartenders, strippers, or watching ESPN on one of the many TVs. In an unusual turn of events, the ladies tended to want to have conversations with me, and I often got numbers. But I made it clear I wasn't interested, due to our lack of common hobbies.

Those nights out did, however, give me more opportunities to meet people. At the bar my team and I would go to after baseball games, I met a wild Jewish girl. She talked to me about everything, from her adventurous sex experience in college, to the subjects she was really passionate about. She was beyond intelligent, and I loved to talk to her about the things I'd learned in college, and during my travels. I remember her telling me that she had never experienced racism because as she said, "My people own everything." It was deep, and I was really heavy into my studies, so I knew about the history of interactions between the Jews and Blacks, meaning the good, the bad, and the ugly. One day, while talking about Egypt, she got mad because she said that the Egyptians enslaved her people, and we never talked after that. Situations similar to this happened periodically, but it was all the same outcome. That's when I realized that I needed to stop wasting time on those scenarios and get focused. I ended up getting married to my first wife: a beautiful, strong-willed smart woman that helped me become more of a man, in more ways than one. She showed me what a woman wants in bed and stepped my sex game up dramatically. The relationship however, came to an end when it was clear I wasn't in the mindset to be married: my immaturity and lack of experience lended to its demise.

Culturally, I completely submerged myself not only into the black conscious community, but into the community of Atlanta as well. I learned that the city has a strong culture of its own. I also started playing rock music again with an all-black Rock band called AMUL9, and with them, shared the stage with bands like Fishbone, Bad brains, and Tribal Seeds. I had also been fortunate enough to play some shows on the road, and even got to record with the drummer of Bad Brains, Earl Hudson. As a result, I have either seen, played with, or am friends with all the musical heroes I looked up to that are still alive. Atlanta was the perfect place for me, because the city was able to cultivate and feed every part of my personality. It is truly the best American city I've had the pleasure of experiencing. The struggle of my past interactions and accepting my black awareness was still there, but Atlanta helped me compromise, and overstand the results of being Bi-cultural. I was groomed to take part in the American dream, but I was unsure what to do once I found out it was all an illusion.

# 8

# Behind The Nine Ball

In my studies, I've read books by a diverse group of authors that helped elevate me to where I am today. Dr. Malachi Z York was an individual that woke me up consciously, and elevated me to a status of self-awareness. I recognized that Black Americans needed to take care of their own, similar to how the Jews, Asians, European, and Arabs have done. Dr. York envisioned us building a community that circulated money and invested it back into our own people and communities. On what was called "Saviors Day" on the "Tama Re," I saw thousands of people, with skin of many different colors come together for a week to peacefully pray, sing, and chant. It was the first time I had ever seen anything like this, and it was organized by Black people. The impact he had on Hip-Hop, and the black conscious community, is unprecedented. With all his teachings, I had three huge takeaways: One, research everything and don't believe anyone; Two, our story is vast and there are specific reasons as to why people do not want us to know ourselves (because of our greatness and potential); Three, the most powerful tool we have is our connection to our ancestors, and nature.

The most profound book I have ever read was a book Dr. York wrote in the late 60's and early 70's called Behind the Nine Ball. The book is a text in which Dr. York provides a blueprint to achieve success for Africans in the Diaspora. This book made me realize the importance of maintaining the African culture within a foreign land: No one can take away your connections to your roots or ancestry. I avoid getting into debates about religion and politics because of these reasons - everyone has their own beliefs that fit into their way of living. It's better to seek to understand multiple perspectives. For example, Islam is not the only right religion (neither is Christianity or Judaism). It does, and has helped millions become better people, but it can also become dangerous when humans begin to interpret the text to fit into their own ideals of what is right and wrong. Other monotheistic religions have similar problems. While they are wonderful tools for individuals to become aware, they are also part of a bigger picture.

For Africans, most older spiritual ways of life

have been diluted to an unrecognizable point. The power that Africans have held, and still hold, is the reason we are feared so much. If we overstood the sciences and ways of life we once had, most of our current issues would not exist. How did the Mahdi beat the British? How did Haiti beat all the major European countries and make them flee from their island? This power that Africans possess was, and still is, a reason why people of color were persecuted in history, even up to this present day. Yet, society attempts to demonize the religions coming from Africa and write it off as Evil, Witchcraft or devil worship. Voodoo is not evil, Ifa is not evil. African spiritual sciences and systems are not evil, rather, they are actually the origins of modern day religion. These traditions pre-date all monotheistic religions, and have influenced them all. Even the ancient Egyptians were working their version of African Spirituality and other forms of African esoteric sciences, to the point that they are now being used daily all across Africa and in the Caribbean today. Remember, we had languages, cultures, and way of life before the oppressors gave us foreign versions of their belief systems, and forcibly instilled them upon us. And we are now the end result of this. We've had access to all the powers in the universe, but were handed a different religion, rooted in a different history, which disconnected us from our powers and our divinity. The result? We are superhumans without the manual to know how to work it. However, we have to start somewhere, and a manual is always the best starting point. I appreciate and respect all religions and religious scriptures. I take from each that which works for me, and leave what doesn't. Our true way of life pre-dates any religion on this planet. There's no need to reinvent the wheel. These systems are here, and they and our ancestors are waiting for us to embrace them.

# 9

# Racism

    We shouldn't even be talking about this subject, but because the mindset and conscious level of this planet has been so low for so long, it would be irresponsible to not address it. It's interesting how racism has manifested itself into our lives and this planet. Racism is a very new concept to humanity, and is something western civilization has brought to us recently. If you're comparing the length of reign of white supremacy or white colonialism to the length of time where people of color ruled the world, particularly Africans, it is impossible to compare with such a difference.

I have always been fascinated by the Nazis, The Vril, theosophical society, and Madam Blavatsky. Obviously I do not agree with the fact of the killing of millions of people or their doctrine of racial superiority. In addition, my Grandmother and her side of the family had Jewish ancestry. All that aside, they intrigued me, but my main focus was on their attraction to the occult and how they tried to tie themselves into ancient cultures. I once watched a documentary that showed how the Nazis were looking for ancient artifacts, and couldn't find any truly ancient artifacts of their own so they started making up their own history. I say this because our stories were placed on stone to stand the test of time, specifically, for the reason that has become a reality today. We forgot who we were and where we came from, and it was done purposely so we could not connect to our greatness, and connect to a time in which we did everything you see happening today.. but on way higher levels. The Moors, the Olmecs, the Egyptians, the Dogons, the Massi, and so many other tribes, were running this globe, and building temples, and structures before the civilized Caucasians were in existence. Racism is new because it came with a new mindset, of a new people, that were given rule over the planet for a certain time frame. One thing people don't realize is that the universe is impartial. Every race has had its day to rule this planet. Every race has had help from whatever you want to call them: GODS, ALIENS, ANGELS, WATCHERS, OVERSEERS and many others. And since every Race is unique in it's own way, no one race is better than another. And ultimately, a race should be gauged by its actions as opposed to anything else. What did the race do to help humanity or hurt humanity? There is a staunch contrast between people that build temples and pyramids over the globe to teach and raise the consciousness level of humanity, as opposed to people that brutalized others for self-gain and monetary advancement. Not to say that all cultures didn't have issues with each other, they did, but in record, the only people to set up this systematic form of slavery that happened to our people was done recently and was done mainly by Caucasians, with the help of Africans and Arabs, I might add. It's very difficult for me to understand racism, because I realize that all humans come from stardust. All humans are connected to one source. The issue is that the mindset of people are so confined, and some people believe the genetic makeup of a person is more important than who that person is and what they've contributed to the world.

We have a wide variety of levels of consciousness that can be encased in a human body. From the very low savage beast, man or woman, to the highest genius and spiritual masters. Sometimes I believe the lack of melanin makes it harder for people to connect to nature. The sun is a power source that strengthens some people and kills others. Why is that? On this physical plane, there are attributes that can only be acquired though millions of years of evolution. Melanin and kinky hair aren't negative traits. They are protection for when Lucy was walking around next to dinosaurs in Africa. Yes, dinosaurs. Africans walked this Earth for far longer than any other civilized race was created or came into existence. Besides a few cases of people on this planet, all races came from Africans. We, for hundreds of thousands of years, were using high sciences, math, and astronomy. We are not niggers, spooks, coons, negroes, apes or any other name. We have to realize that we were once worshipped as gods, but as all cycles go, we have reached the lowest point of the evolutionary scale, and are now making our way back. It is a process and will take time but our awakening is inevitable. It will see us leaving our patriarchal society and embracing our original Matriarchal society. And once the woman is put back in her original, leadership role, things will change. We are witnessing a small example today, with so many women taking congressional seats in American politics.

We may be different genetically, but we are still only one human race. A lot of white people I have come across are not racist, don't agree with racism, and despise what has been done to people of color. And those that think any differently, are becoming a smaller and smaller minority. Why waste time hating another person, for no reason? I overstand why, because I've seen the mindset that hates, but I don't believe it's natural. Racism is unnatural, in its very form. We only give it power because we agree to be a part of this system. Some think racism will end if all races go back to where they came from: Caucasian Americans back to Europe, Asians back to Asia, and so on. But we all know how unrealistic that sounds. Instead, people need to know that for all of us, our physical make up consists of the same stardust. That's it: Small containers, holding a part of the source, in a human body made of stardust. We are connected both physically, and spiritually.

# 10

# America, The Great Divide

One of the primary factors behind the divide in the American society has been the fact that there are two major American identities that are fighting for power. To understand these identities, we have to start from the beginning.

The original inhabitants of America are Black Africans. The Native Americans, and similar indigenous groups around the globe are a mixture of Mongoloids and Negroids. Asians and Africans came together and made a new race in which you call Indians, Latinos, or Mexicans. As such, the Africans and Indians are our Native Americans. This is evident not only by the prejudice they experienced but even less significant items like clothing. The Native Americans wore clothing that resembled pieces originating in Egypt, such as the headdress and arpon. There is a similarity between animal representation and spiritual practices among both groups as well. Fast-forward to slavery, and there's the added result of black slaves mixing into Native

American tribes when they attempted to escape. The back-stories of all these groups are similar too. Colonizers came and stole their land, changed their names, their culture, insulted their spiritual systems, then replaced it with their way of life.

This Euro-America was an experiment that melanated people had no say in, but had to help build regardless. This America was not originally made for people of color. We were 'The Help', and after years of constant debate between the citizens of this country, we have reached a point of a second civil war: The white nationalists want their country back, to restore it to one that reflects the ideals they believe their forefathers had for this nation. This is as ridiculous as trying to send everyone back to their place of origin, because between integration and multiculturalism, many American people have come to embrace this new culture and way of life. There are now generations of mixed race people, and separating them would be impossible. How can there be a race war when, in some cases, our extended and immediate families are from different races? This is the direction America is already headed.

One 'American identity' refers to those that want to return to the social rules and accepted behavior of George Washington's era. The other identity, they overstand the idea of moving forward and embracing new ideas and cultures. I realized that being exposed to more cultures increases tolerance, and the most intolerant people are those that have not experienced many differences, be it races, religions, or cultures.

I think back to the children I saw in my neighborhood. These children were of different races, and participated in activities together, and soon formed a diverse crew. They all grew up playing sports together, went to high-school together, married interracially, and have remained friends to this day. All it took was some early introduction to different races, and these children are vastly different than the ones that only spent time around people of their own race. In fact, one of these kids had a brother I went to school with; I even got a ride to school with him and his sister: He's now a state trooper, and, I hope I'm wrong, but knowing this system, he's probably a typical racist policeman patrolling the streets giving people of color a hard time. His little brother, on the other hand, was a part of a different crew, and ended up marrying a person of Asian descent. This is the current state of America and where it is headed, the third version of it. This country will never go back to it's past. The cycles of time will not allow this regression, no matter how bad people want it. There is a whole new level of consciousness that is happening here on this planet, and it will ultimately consume the minds and spirits of the people inhabiting it. This is inevitable, and there is no way to stop it. Again, we are witnessing the last stand of these outdated mindsets here in America, and those mindsets will not go out, without a fight. Just like the Honorable Antonio Montana (Scarface/Al Pacino) said, "Every Dog has its Day."

# 11

# Black Wall Street

When I first read about Black Wall Street, I almost jumped out the window with excitement. I was so immensely impressed by the feats of my ancestors. In school, the edited-dictation (education) teaches us that Black Americans did nothing but pick cotton and do strenuous amounts of labor for no pay. It was incredible to learn about the economic independence American Blacks adapted to during segregation. They actually made it work for themselves! But if that was the case, why didn't the nation leave Blacks alone at that point? If they wanted segregation, and everyone seemed to be prospering separately, then what was the problem? Once a people get empowered financially and become self-reliant, it becomes very hard to oppress them, and use them to make money. As a result, today, we don't understand how to become financially independent, and we are forced to throw our money at other races. The American school system does not teach our children about economics and business in the same way that, other races, can learn about these vital things from relatives. We have no financial learning structure to pass down to future generations, which puts us behind Asians, Arabs, and Caucasians, groups that have had a monopoly on this information until recently. The power of the internet has given us more access to this knowledge. Our ancestors showed how it can be done, and fortunately, more and more Black Americans are learning these business tactics, and spreading them to the community.

For as long as the Black race has been walking this Earth, we depended on each other for survival. However, the world has changed to put Blacks worldwide at a disadvantage, creating an agenda for us to fuel the economy while getting little in return. We rely on handouts from a government that has shown animosity and disdain towards us for years. To counter this, we should be creating communities around the world that encourage spreading money between our brothers and sisters. Every great leader, the Honorable Elijah Muhhamad, Marcus Garvey, Noble Drew Ali, Yawheh Ben Yahweh, Minister Farrakan, and Dr. York, have all urged for us to spend our own money, on our own people. If we truly want freedom as a people, then financial freedom is one of the first keys that will open the door. Can we resurrect a Nubian Wall Street from state to state, island to island, and link it to our mother continent? I think with the bright minds we have today, this could easily become a reality.

Now comes the issue of blending black consciousness and the American illusion. For me, bi-cultural means having two lives within one reality, which I think is the conflict a lot of Black Americans are feeling right now. It's hard to pick and choose what to accept as truth and what to throw away as fiction, especially when we're all accustomed to living the American dream. I'm grateful to have grown up in this country and experienced all the liberties and rights that came with it - I would never want to change that. Our reality is so diverse, and we have all dealt with different experiences growing up. Some of us might have been raised in areas like Virginia, where it's clear Black Americans are the minority. However, others were raised in the hearts of places like Atlanta, where the demographic shift makes you the majority where you reside. These differences will give you a different experience, and it will influence how you coexist and your tolerance for differences, such as race, religion, political affiliation, and sexual orientation. Regardless of our different paths in life, we are all dealing with the present issues that plague Black Americans. We are in fear of our children being discriminated against, or losing their lives to white supremacists masquerading as police officers. The safest option is for us to create our own environments and institutions. There is no excuse why we can't put our resources together and build for ourselves. Unfortunately, the American side in us has made it difficult to break out of the slave mentality. We face adverse forces that continually push us against the mindset for liberation. If true world history was taught, and we were to see ourselves for who we really are, we would have a completely different outlook on what we are actually capable of. The struggle is over, and it's time for us to take back our birth-right as the indigenous people on this planet as the majority, not the minority. Once an individual opens themselves to this mindset, they begin to see a grander scheme of things. There are so many basic things we do today, that would change, once we embrace our original way of life. Things such as: eating correctly, praying correctly, using nature to help protect and heal when necessary, and reaching out to our ancestors for guidance. One key element to embracing an 'Indigenous mindset' is that it instills in us an automatic connection to nature. And with that, comes a respect for animals, nature and people, which then shifts the main focus of one's life towards a path of elevating one-self, the people around you, and the surrounding environment. This is the major difference between the mindset of today in comparison to our ancient ancestors.

Ultimately, living a bi-cultural existence is all about maintaining balance. I have had the experience and overstanding of how it is being a Black American in America. But also, to embrace my indigenous mindset; to unlock my true being, and I am in the process of elevating myself to this highest status. There is nothing wrong with watching an American sport's game and doing an African ritual for prosperity, all within the same day. We have the mental freedom to switch between African roots, and embracing American fun. Conflict occurs when someone disrupts our mental freedom. In fact, many issues that humanity has faced were the result of GroupThink: The problem of racism is an example of this. But we are now in a time in which the consciousness level of all of humanity will elevate. It is inevitable.

Think about your own mindset and the closest people around you. Would you say you, and most of your immediate friends and family are racist, sexist or homophobic? Do you think it's okay to hate or discriminate against anyone of these people? Probably not, because as a group we are steadily elevating to a level, one that understands how to treat people better. Often times, those who escape the hold of group-think and shift to more negative perspectives are dealing with insecurity, so they heighten themselves by putting down others. A Caucasian friend asked me why I posts about 'Black Power' on social media. I had to explain to her that when Black people talk about 'Black Power' it is geared towards self-empowerment, building community, and uplifting the mindset and integrity of a person. It is not about killing white people or hating other races just because they look different. Doing so would put us on the same level as the people that committed atrocities against our race for so many years. Instead, we should protect ourselves and our families from the actions of this mindset. But we shouldn't yield to it. Black power, quite simply, is Black Wall Street, Timbuktu, Ancient Africa, and Egypt. Even the fictional world of Wakanda is a display of Black excellence. It is what we want to achieve for our people. And the better we are as a community, the better relations we have with the rest of the world. This is inevitable, as well. There is no way to equate the White power and White supremacist mindset to Black power: the ideals are rooted in a mindset of self-empowerment, as opposed to having inferiority or superiority complexes.

When colonialism took over, it was with the mindset of Manifest Destiny. In a way, this made sense. It was a time in the cycle for a certain race to rule, and ultimately, like all before them, they have an expiration date. Personally, I think every race should be proud of who they are, and be able to represent, and show pride to the fullest capacity. As a fellow human being, I can marvel at the great things that other races have accomplished. Why wouldn't I? Knowing one's past, and what our ancestors accomplished is fulfilling. However, to flaunt what my ancestors were able to accomplish, while looking down at others, would be ridiculous. This book is about my own people and their greatness, so the focus is on them. However, this does not mean I don't acknowledge the many triumphs of other races. Despite my bad experiences with Caucasians, I've had a lot of great times! Speaking honestly, people are people and if it seems impossible to respect someone for being different, then leave them alone. There's no need to necessarily like them, but at least respect them as a fellow human being. We should judge others only by their accomplishments and works, not by sexuality, gender, race, or any other factors that don't contribute to who they are as a person. To help you, the reader, understand what I mean, I have a story to share:

My brother had a rare kidney disorder. As time progressed, he lost functions in his kidneys, and eventually had to go on dialysis. As a family, we all tried to be donors, but we weren't compatible for numerous reasons. When I was in Richmond, I would go visit my brother at Radford college where he was a member of a fraternity. One weekend I met this guy named Liam, who I later found out played T-ball back in Maryland, and was on the same team as my brother back when they were children. Well, after graduating college, Liam, my brother, and his wife, decided to live together once they moved to Atlanta. Liam being from the DMV (D.C, Maryland, and Virginia), was into punk rock, and always supported me and my music. He funded my very first demo for Amul9; paid for it in full, and didn't ask for a dime back. Liam had moved to Portland,

Oregon with his family, but knew what the situation was with my brother, and took the compatibility donor test as well. Well ladies and gentlemen, this Irish guy with no hair and no melanin was an exact match for my brother. I'm not exaggerating, Liam looked like he could be a stunt double for Remey (Michael Rappaport) in Higher Learning. So Liam briefly flew back to Atlanta, gave my brother a kidney, and the rest is history. This human being didn't need to do this, but he did it because his brother needed him and cared about him. Two kids coming together as fate ordained, and now one life is back to normal because of one word, "LOVE."
Antidote for Racism
#AFR

With that being said, love yourself, love your family, love your race, love your culture, love your neighbor, and ultimately be the best person you can be, and share that with the next generation. We are all human, one family, and should always look out and care for each other. Once we overstand the changes that will inevitably aid our continued survival, we will all be in a better position on this planet we call home. We are coming into the age of Aquarius, and an awakening will occur amongst all of the human race. I thank you for taking the time to read this.

Peace and love, my human family.

Mus Zoser Ankh Hat

## Book Reccomendations

Author: Cheikh Anta Diop
Book: The African Origin of Civilization: Myth Or Reality

Author: Don Miguel Ruiz
Books(s): The Four Agreements

Author: Dr. Malachi Z York
Books(s): Behind The Nine Ball, The Holy Tablets, The Mind, Sacred Wisdom of Tehuti, The Black Book
Author: Hannibal B. Johnson
Books(s): Black Wall Street: From Riot to book

Author: Helena Petrovna Blavatsky
Books(s): The Secret Doctrine series

Author: Ivan Van Sertima
Book(s): They Came Before Columbus: The African Presence in Ancient America, The Golden Age of the Moor, Ancient Future, and many more titles.

Author: Robert Bauval
Books(s): Origins of the Sphinx: Celestial Guardian of Pre-Pharaonic Civilization, Secret Chamber Revisited: The Quest for the Lost Knowledge of Ancient Egypt, Vatican Heresy: Bernini and the Building of the Hermetic Temple of the Sun, and many more titles.

Author: The Honorable Elijah Muhammad
Book(s): How To Eat To Live, The Fall of America, Message to the BlackMan, and many more titles.

Author: Zecharia Sitchin
Book(s): A series of books with the newest being, The Anunnaki Chronicles

## Bibliography

Ackwerh, Sarah. Dogon Tribe of Mali. Face2Face Africa, 28 June 2018, https://face2faceafrica.com/article/the-astronomical-knowledge-of-the-dogon-tribe-of-mali-dating-back-to-3200-bc

Cheikh Anta Diop. Wikipedia, 30 Aug. 2019, https://en.wikipedia.org/wiki/Cheikh_Anta_Diop

"Ivan Van Sertima." Journal of African Civilizations, 2017, http://www.journalofafricancivilizations.com/VanSertima

Knapp, Wilfred F., et al. Adolf Hitler. Encyclopaedia Britannica, 3 May 2019, https://www.britannica.com/biography/Adolf-Hitler

Malik, Asad. "Dr. Malachi Z York Founder of the Nuwaubian Nation." The Pan-African Alliance, 24 Sept. 2018, https://www.panafricanalliance.com/dr-malachi-z-york-nuwaubian-nation-of-moors/

Robinson, B.A. A man practicing Vodun. Religious Tolerance, 7 Feb. 2010, http://www.religioustolerance.org/voodoo.htm

Sitchin, J. Zecharia Sitchin. The Official Website of Zecharia Sitchin, 20 Nov. 2017, http://www.sitchin.com/

The Editors of Encyclopaedia Britannica. Helena Blavatsky. Encyclopaedia Britannica, 8 Aug. 2019, https://www.britannica.com/biography/Helena-Blavatsky

"The Honorable Elijah Muhammad." Nation of Islam, 2018, https://www.noi.org/honorable-elijah-muhammad/

www.ingramcontent.com/pod-product-compliance
Lightning Source LLC
Chambersburg PA
CBHW020430010526
44118CB00010B/517